ANGELS

ANGELS

A JOYOUS CELEBRATION

COURAGE BOOKS

AN IMPRINT OF RUNNING PRESS
PHILADELPHIA • LONDON

9   8   7   6   5   4   3   2
Digit on the right indicates the number of this printing.
Library of Congress Cataloging-in-Publication number 96-67156
ISBN 1-56138-743-6

Cover and interior design by Maria Taffera Lewis
Quotes researched by Joan McIntosh
Introduction by Kristin Cuddihy
Edited by Elaine M. Bucher
Pictures researched by Susan Oyama

Published by Courage Books, an imprint of
Running Press Book Publishers
125 South Twenty-second Street
Philadelphia, Pennsylvania 19103-4399

Contents

INTRODUCTION

A WORLD WITHOUT ANGELS WOULD BE A WORLD WITHOUT HOPE. ANGELS APPEAR IN THE EARLIEST STORIES OF OUR EXISTENCE—WINGED CREATURES THAT BELONG TO A HIGHER ORDER THAN MAN. ANGELS ARE DEPICTED AS MESSENGERS, MUSICIANS, GUARDIANS, CUPIDS, AND EVEN WARRIORS. THE ANGEL IS A BRIDGE BETWEEN HEAVEN AND EARTH, A HUMAN FORM WITH DIVINE ALTERATIONS—WINGS, HALOS, AND GOLDEN AURAS. THEY ARE DIVINE MESSENGERS WITH GRACE AND ARCHETYPAL BEAUTY OR ROBUST YOUTHS WITH BOW AND ARROW OR HARP AND FLUTE. SOME OF THE GREATEST PAINTERS AND SCULPTORS IN THE HISTORY OF ART HAVE DEALT WITH THE IMAGE OF THE ANGEL. EACH ARTIST BROUGHT TO HIS RENDERING A COMBINATION OF THE TRADITIONAL IMAGE AND A PERSONAL VISION. THIS COMBINATION OF THE UNIQUE AND THE COMMON HAS PRODUCED SOME OF THE WORLD'S FINEST WORKS OF ART.

◆

A N G E L S

The Greeks and Romans saw the angel as an allegory for divine wisdom or powers. Statues and frescoes commemorating triumph almost always used a winged figure to represent victory. The winged cupid represented the duality of love; the lovely, playful cherub wielded a bow and arrow in order to pierce the heart of his intended.

With the rise of Christianity angels became icons of divine perfection—they were beautiful, graceful, loyal servants who performed varied services for the Almighty. They began to inhabit religious paintings in increasing numbers and in prominent positions. By the early Renaissance, the angel had become a favorite subject in painting, immortalized in the sublime perfection of works by artists such as Botticelli and Raphael.

The art of the post-Renaissance began a slow return to the secular world and its scenes, but angels remained a lasting symbol of the presence of the divine in our earthly realm. Angels continue to inhabit the conscience of our culture. They are not only part of our religious world but are also part of our popular literature, myth, and fantasy. Angels are a reminder to us all of our potential for perfection. They are the guardians of our well-being and serve as inspirations and examples of grace, happiness, and harmony. The more materialistic our world becomes, the more we embrace the idea that angels watch over us and change our lives.

GUARDIANS

F or God will deign

To visit oft the dwellings of just men

Delighted, and with frequent intercourse

Thither will send his winged messengers

On errands of supernatural grace.

John Milton (1608–1674)
English poet

He shall give his angels charge over thee,

to keep thee in all thy ways.

Psalm 91:11
The Bible

♦
11

THE ANGELS . . . REGARD OUR SAFETY,

UNDERTAKE OUR DEFENSE, DIRECT OUR WAYS,

AND EXERCISE A CONSTANT SOLICITUDE

THAT NO EVIL BEFALL US.

John Calvin (1509–1564)
French theologian and reformer

The guardian angels of life sometimes

fly so high as to be beyond our sight,

but they are always looking down upon us.

JEAN PAUL RICHTER (1763-1825)
FRENCH WRITER AND HUMORIST

I'VE HEARD THAT LITTLE INFANTS CONVERSE BY SMILES AND SIGNS

WITH THE GUARDIAN BAND OF ANGELS THAT ROUND THEM SHINES,

UNSEEN BY GROSSER SENSES; BELOVED ONE! DOST THOU

SMILE SO UPON THY HEAVENLY FRIENDS, AND COMMUNE WITH THEM NOW?

Caroline Anne Southey (1786–1854)
English poet

I have seen angels by the sick one's pillow;

Their's was the soft tone and the soundless tread,

Where smitten hearts were drooping like the willow,

They stood 'between the living and the dead.'

Unknown

FOUR ANGELS TO MY BED,

FOUR ANGELS ROUND MY HEAD,

ONE TO WATCH AND ONE TO PRAY

AND TWO TO BEAR MY SOUL AWAY.

Thomas Ady
17th-century English writer

Beside each man who's born on earth

A guardian angel takes his stand,

To guide him through life's mysteries. . . .

Menander of Athens (c. 343–291 B.C.)
Greek playwright and poet

WHEN TEMPTED, INVOKE YOUR ANGEL.

HE IS MORE EAGER TO HELP YOU THAN YOU ARE TO BE HELPED!

IGNORE THE DEVIL AND DO NOT BE AFRAID OF HIM:

HE TREMBLES AND FLEES AT YOUR GUARDIAN ANGEL'S SIGHT.

St. John Basco [Giovanni Melchior] (1815–1888)
Italian priest and writer

◆

21

THERE ARE TWO ANGELS, THAT ATTEND UNSEEN

EACH ONE OF US, AND IN GREAT BOOKS RECORD

OUR GOOD AND EVIL DEEDS. HE WHO WRITE DOWN

THE GOOD ONES, AFTER EVERY ACTION CLOSES

HIS VOLUME, AND ASCENDS WITH IT TO GOD.

THE OTHER KEEPS HIS DREADFUL DAY-BOOK OPEN

TILL SUNSET, THAT WE MAY REPENT; WHICH DOING,

THE RECORD OF THE ACTION FADES AWAY,

AND LEAVES A LINE OF WHITE ACROSS THE PAGE.

Henry Wadsworth Longfellow (1807–1882)
American poet

Abou Ben Adhem (may his tribe increase)!
Awoke one night from a deep dream of peace,

And saw, within the moonlight in his room,
Making it rich, and like a lily in bloom,

An angel writing in a book of gold:
Exceeding peace had made Ben Adhem bold,

And to the Presence in the room he said,
What writest thou?" The Vision raised its head,

And with a look made of all sweet accord
Answered, "The names of those who love the Lord,"

"And is mine one?" said Abou. "Nay, not so,"
Replied the Angel. Abou spoke more low,

But cheerily still; and said, "I pray thee, then,
Write me as one that loves his fellow-men."

The Angel wrote, and vanished. The next night
It came again with a great wakening light,

And showed the names whom love of God had blessed,
And, lo! Ben Adhem's name led all the rest.

LEIGH HUNT (1784–1859)
ENGLISH WRITER

♦

When children lay them down to sleep,

Two angels come, their watch to keep,

Cover them up, safely and warm,

Tenderly shield them from ev'ry harm.

But when they wake at dawn of day,

The two bright angels go away,

Rest from their work of care and love

For God Himself keeps watch above.

❦

Unknown

Henry Fuseli 1741–1825   The Apotheosis of Penelope Boothby   Cheadle Gift

If there be for him an angel,

an intercessor, one among a thousand,

to vouch for man's uprightness,

then He is gracious.

Job 33:23
The Bible

We should pray to the angels, for they are given to us as guardians.

St. Ambrose (c. 340–397)
Italian bishop

♦

29

ANGELS

. . . with beautiful wings of silk and crowns of baby rose-

buds. . . . all live together in a castle . . . and when the angels want to go

someplace they just whistle—and a cloud floats to the castle door and picks them

up. And the angels ride through the sky riding the cloud like a magic carpet—under

the moon and through the stars—until they're right above us. That's how they can

look down and see if we're all right—and sometimes even send messages to us.

FROM THE MOVIE *THE LITTLE PRINCESS*

◆

ANGELS OF LOVE

U NLESS YOU CAN LOVE, AS THE ANGELS MAY,

  WITH THE BREATH OF HEAVEN BETWIXT YOU. . . .

OH, NEVER CALL IT LOVING!

Elizabeth Barrett Browning (1806–1861)
English poet

Love's heralds should be thoughts

Which ten times faster glide than the sun's beams

Driving back shadows over low'ring hills;

Therefore do nimble-pinion'd doves draw love;

And therefore hath the wind-swift Cupid wings.

WILLIAM SHAKESPEARE (1564–1616)
ENGLISH PLAYWRIGHT AND POET

Her beautiful hair

dropped over me—

like an angel's wing.

CHARLES DICKENS (1812–1870)
ENGLISH WRITER

LOVE

I imagine the leathery sound of wings—not bats

but angels lighting down, naked, gorgeous.

ROBERT FERRO (1941–1988)
AMERICAN WRITER

O Lyric Love,

HALF ANGEL AND HALF BIRD,

AND ALL A WONDER

AND A WILD DESIRE.

Robert Browning (1812–1889)
English poet

ANGELS

STONE WALLS DO NOT A PRISON MAKE,

NOR IRON BARS A CAGE;

MINDS INNOCENT AND QUIET TAKE

THAT FOR A HERMITAGE;

IF I HAVE FREEDOM IN MY LOVE,

AND IN SOUL AM FREE,

ANGELS ALONE THAT SOAR ABOVE

ENJOY SUCH LIBERTY.

Richard Lovelace (1618–1657)
English poet

Self is the only prison that can ever find the soul;

Love is the only angel who can bid the gates unroll;

And when he comes to call thee, arise and follow fast;

His way may lie through darkness, but it leads to light at last.

HENRY VAN DYKE (1822–1891)
AMERICAN CLERIC AND WRITER

ANGELS

ANGELS LISTEN WHEN SHE SPEAKS: SHE'S MY DELIGHT, ALL MANKIND'S WONDER. . . .

John Wilmot Rochester (1647–1680)

English poet

I feel as if it would be flattering an angel to compare

such a creature to you. You have been privileged to receive

every gift from nature, you have both fortitude and tears.

VICTOR HUGO (1802-1885)
FRENCH WRITER

SHE WAS A PHANTOM OF DELIGHT

WHEN FIRST SHE GLEAMED UPON MY SIGHT;

A LOVELY APPARITION . . .

AND YET A SPIRIT STILL AND BRIGHT,

WITH SOMETHING OF AN ANGEL LIGHT.

William Wordsworth (1770-1850)
English poet

. . . he fell asleep, and dreamed he saw her

coming bounding towards him, just as she used to come,

with a wreath of jessamine in her hair, her cheeks

bright, and her eyes radiant with delight;

but, as he looked, she seemed to rise from the ground;

her cheeks wore a paler hue—her eyes had a deep,

divine radiance, a golden halo seemed around her head

—and she vanished from his sight. . . .

Harriet Beecher Stowe (1811–1896)
American writer

WHEN LOVE SPEAKS, THE VOICE OF ALL THE GODS

MAKES HEAVEN DROWSY WITH THE HARMONY.

William Shakespeare (1564–1616)
English playwright and poet

♦

O

F ALL EARTHLY MUSIC

THAT WHICH REACHES FARTHEST

INTO HEAVEN IS THE BEATING

OF A TRULY LOVING HEART.

Henry Ward Beecher (1813–1887)
American cleric

There is music even in the beauty, and the silent note which Cupid strikes,

far sweeter than the sound of an instrument.

THOMAS BROWNE (1605–1682)
ENGLISH PHYSICIAN AND WRITER

EVERY SAINT IN HEAVEN IS AS A FLOWER

IN THE GARDEN OF GOD, AND HOLY LOVE IS THE FRAGRANCE

AND SWEET ODOR THAT THEY ALL SEND FORTH, AND

WITH WHICH THEY FILL THE BOWERS OF THAT PARADISE ABOVE.

EVERY SOUL THERE IS, IS A NOTE IN SOME CONCERT

OF DELIGHTFUL MUSIC, THAT SWEETLY HARMONIZES

WITH EVERY OTHER NOTE, AND ALL TOGETHER BLEND

IN THE MOST RAPTUROUS STRAINS. . . .

Jonathan Edwards (1703–1758)
American cleric and theologian

EARTHLY ANGELS

THE WORLD HAS ANGELS ALL TOO FEW,

AND HEAVEN IS OVERFLOWING.

Samuel Taylor Coleridge (1772–1834)
English poet and critic

Angels are in the heavens, I am sure, because there are deeds done by mortals

that are difficult to explain by the mortal nature of man. The angels of self-sacrifice

and everlasting devotion, of courage and tenderness—they must be fluttering about

in the winds high above, sometimes taking on the face of man and his flesh.

DAGOBERT D. RUNES (1902-1982)
AMERICAN WRITER

MILLIONS OF SPIRITUAL CREATURES WALK THE EARTH

UNSEEN, BOTH WHEN WE WAKE AND WHEN WE SLEEP.

John Milton (1608–1674)
English poet

57

BE NOT FORGETFUL TO ENTERTAIN STRANGERS, FOR

THEREBY SOME HAVE ENTERTAINED ANGELS UNAWARES.

Hebrews 13:2
The Bible

If angels are entertained unaware, it is because they have tact.

SPENCER BAYNE (1899–1978)
AMERICAN WRITER

IF SOME PEOPLE REALLY SEE ANGELS WHERE OTHERS SEE ONLY EMPTY SPACE,

LET THEM PAINT THE ANGELS. . . .

John Ruskin (1819–1900)
English critic and writer

Outside the open window

The morning air is all awash with angels.

RICHARD PURDY WILBUR (B.1921)
AMERICAN POET

AND WITH THE MORN, THOSE ANGEL FACES SMILE

WHICH I HAVE LOVED LONG SINCE, AND LOST AWHILE.

John Henry Newman (1801–1890)
English theologian and cardinal

•

He passed the flaming bounds of place and time:

The living throne, the sapphire-blaze,

Where angels tremble, while they gaze,

He saw; but blasted with excess of light,

Closed his eyes in endless night.

Thomas Gray (1716–1771)
English poet

In this dim world of clouding cares,

We rarely know, till 'wildered eyes

See white wings lessening up the skies,

The angels with us unawares.

Gerald Massey (1828–1907)
English poet

•

O welcome, pure-ey'd Faith, white-handed Hope,

Thou hovering angel, girt with golden wings!

JOHN MILTON (1608–1674)

ENGLISH POET

THE ONLY THING WE ARE MISSING IS ANGELS. IN THIS VAST WORLD THERE IS NO PLACE FOR THEM. AND ANYWAY, WOULD OUR EYES RECOGNIZE THEM? PERHAPS WE ARE SURROUNDED BY ANGELS WITHOUT KNOWING IT.

Henry Miller (1891–1980)
American writer

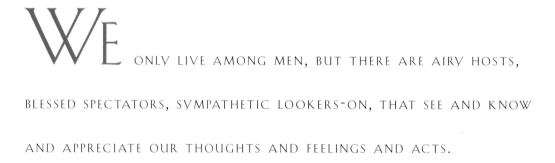

WE ONLY LIVE AMONG MEN, BUT THERE ARE AIRY HOSTS, BLESSED SPECTATORS, SYMPATHETIC LOOKERS-ON, THAT SEE AND KNOW AND APPRECIATE OUR THOUGHTS AND FEELINGS AND ACTS.

Henry Ward Beecher (1813–1887)
American cleric

MUSICAL MESSENGERS

Music soothes us, stirs us up; it puts noble feelings in us; it melts us to tears,

we know not how:—it is a language by itself,

just as perfect, in its way, as speech, as words; just as divine, just as blessed. . . .

CHARLES KINGSLEV (1819–1875)
ENGLISH CLERIC AND WRITER

MUSIC

Music is well said to be the speech of angels:

in fact, nothing among the utterances allowed to man

is felt to be so divine. It brings us near to the infinite.

THOMAS CARLYLE (1795–1881)
SCOTTISH WRITER AND HISTORIAN

In Heaven a spirit doth dwell

       Whose heart-strings are a lute—

None sing so wild—so well

       As the angel Israfel—

And the giddy stars are mute.

EDGAR ALLAN POE (1809–1949)
AMERICAN WRITER AND POET

•

75

Let but the voice engender the string,

And angels will be borne, while thou dost sing.

ROBERT HERRICK (1591–1674)
ENGLISH POET

WHERE THE BRIGHT SERAPHIM IN BURNING ROW

THEIR LOUD UP-LIFTED ANGEL TRUMPETS BLOW.

John Milton (1608–1674)
English poet

The angels were all singing out of tune,

And hoarse with having little else to do,

Excepting to wind up the sun and moon

Or curb a runaway young star or two.

GEORGE GORDON, LORD BYRON (1788–1824)
ENGLISH POET

WHETHER THE ANGELS PLAY ONLY BACH IN PRAISING GOD I AM NOT QUITE SURE;

I AM SURE HOWEVER, THAT *EN FAMILLE* THEY PLAY MOZART.

Karl Barth (1886–1968)
Swiss theologian and educator

So is music an asylum. It takes us out of the actual and whispers

to us dim secrets that startle our wonder as to who we are,

and for what, whence and whereto. All the great interrogatories,

like questioning angels, float in on its waves of sound.

Ralph Waldo Emerson (1803–1882)
American writer and poet

. . . Look how the floor of heaven

       Is thick inlaid with patinas of bright gold;

There's not the smallest orb which thou behold'st

       But in his motion like an angel sings,

Still quiring to the young-ey'd cherubins;

       Such harmony is in immortal souls. . . .

WILLIAM SHAKESPEARE (1564–1616)
ENGLISH PLAYWRIGHT AND POET

◆

Omay I join the choir invisible

Of those immortal dead who live again

In minds made better by their presence: live

In pulses stirred to generosity,

In deeds of daring rectitude, in scorn

For miserable aims that end with self,

In thoughts sublime that pierce the night like stars,

And with their mild persistence urge man's search

To vaster issues.

So to live is heaven;

To make the undying music in the world!

George Eliot [Mary Ann Evans] (1819–1880)
English writer

◆

Ave gracia
plena
dominus ner

HEAVENLY BEINGS

IF GOD COULD MAKE ANGELS, WHY DID HE BOTHER WITH MEN?

Dagobert D. Runes (1902–1982)

American writer

On the second day, God created the angels, with their natural

propensity to good. Later He made beasts with their animal desires.

But God was pleased with neither. So He fashioned man,

a combination of angel and beast, free to follow good or evil.

Midrash Semak
Hebrew biblical text

THERE IS A SPIRITUAL LIFE THAT WE SHARE WITH THE ANGELS

OF HEAVEN AND WITH THE DIVINE SPIRITS, FOR LIKE THEM

WE HAVE BEEN FORMED IN THE IMAGE AND LIKENESS OF GOD.

Lawrence of Brindisi (1559–1619)
Italian religious leader and writer

THEN, IN SUCH HOUR OF NEED

OF YOUR FAINTING, DISPIRITED RACE,

YE, LIKE ANGELS, APPEAR,

RADIANT WITH ARDOR DIVINE.

BEACONS OF HOPE, YE APPEAR!

LANGUOR IS NOT IN YOUR HEART,

WEAKNESS IS NOT IN YOUR WORD,

WEARINESS IS NOT ON YOUR BROW.

Matthew Arnold (1822–1888)
English poet and critic

For compassion a human heart suffices; but for full

and adequate sympathy with joy an angel's only.

SAMUEL TAYLOR COLERIDGE (1772–1834)
ENGLISH POET AND CRITIC

THE EARTH IS TO THE SUN

WHAT MAN IS TO THE ANGELS.

VICTOR HUGO (1802–1885)

FRENCH WRITER

ONE OF THE HARDEST LESSONS WE HAVE TO

LEARN IN THIS LIFE . . . IS TO SEE THE DIVINE,

THE CELESTIAL, THE PURE IN THE COMMON,

THE NEAR AT HAND—TO SEE THAT HEAVEN LIES

ABOUT US HERE IN THIS WORLD.

John Burroughs (1837–1921)
American writer and naturalist

If a man is called to be a streetsweeper, he should sweep streets even as Michelangelo painted, or Beethoven composed music, or Shakespeare wrote poetry. He should sweep streets so well that all the host of heaven and earth will pause to say, here lived a great streetsweeper who did his job well.

MARTIN LUTHER KING, JR. (1929–1968)
AMERICAN CIVIL RIGHTS LEADER AND MINISTER

In pride, in reas'ning pride, our error lies;

All quit their sphere, and rush into the skies!

Pride still is aiming at the bless'd abodes,

Men would be Angels, Angels would be Gods.

Aspiring to be Gods the Angels fell,

Aspiring to be Angels men rebel.

Alexander Pope (1688–1744)
English poet

BUT MAN, PROUD MAN,

DRESS'D IN A LITTLE BRIEF AUTHORITY,

MOST IGNORANT OF WHAT HE'S MOST ASSUR'D,

HIS GLASSY ESSENCE, LIKE AN ANGRY APE,

PLAYS SUCH FANTASTIC TRICKS BEFORE HIGH HEAVEN

AS MAKES THE ANGELS WEEP.

William Shakespeare (1564–1616)
English playwright and poet

How fading are the joys we dote upon!

Like apparitions seen and gone.

But those which soonest take their flight

Are the exquisite and strong—

Like angels' visits, short and bright;

Mortality's too weak to bear them long.

John Norris (1657–1711)
English philosopher and cleric

H

APPY THOSE EARLY DAYS, WHEN I

SHIN'D IN MY ANGEL-INFANCY.

BEFORE I UNDERSTOOD THIS PLACE

APPOINTED FOR MY SECOND RACE,

OR TAUGHT MY SOUL TO FANCY AUGHT

BUT A WHITE CELESTIAL THOUGHT;

WHEN YET I HAD NOT WALKED ABOVE

A MILE OR TWO FROM MY FIRST LOVE,

AND LOOKING BACK—AT THAT SHORT SPACE—

COULD SEE A GLIMPSE OF HIS BRIGHT FACE.

Henry Vaughn (1622–1695)
English poet

Where did you come from, Baby dear?

Out of the everywhere into here. . . .

Whence that three-cornered smile of bliss?

Three angels gave me at once a kiss. . . .

Feet, whence did you come, you darling things?

From the same box as the cherubs' wings. . . .

GEORGE MACDONALD (1824–1905)
SCOTTISH WRITER AND POET

I SHOULD LIKE TO HAVE HAD AN ANGELIC BRUSH, OR FORMS OF PARADISE TO FASHION THE ARCHANGEL, AND TO SEE HIM IN HEAVEN, BUT I HAVE NOT BEEN ABLE TO RISE SO HIGH, AND IN VAIN I HAVE SEARCHED FOR HIM ON EARTH. SO THAT I HAVE LOOKED UPON THAT FORM WHICH I HAVE ESTABLISHED FOR MYSELF IN THE *IDEA*.

GUIDO RENI (1575–1642)
ITALIAN ARTIST

•

I WANT TO BE AN ANGEL,

AND WITH THE ANGELS STAND,

A CROWN UPON MY FOREHEAD,

A HARP WITHIN MY HAND.

Urania Bailey (1820–1882)
American evangelist and writer

I have been on the verge of being an angel

all my life, but it's never happened yet.

MARK TWAIN (1835–1910)
AMERICAN WRITER

EVERY MAN CONTEMPLATES AN ANGEL IN HIS FUTURE SELF.

Ralph Waldo Emerson (1803–1882)
American writer and poet

CELESTIAL MYSTERIES

My aunt used to say: "Always keep yourself on the side of the angels."

It was only after she died that I began to wonder what that meant.

❧

Sue Grafton (b. 1940)

American writer

◆

An angel can illumine the thought

and mind of man by strengthening the power

of vision, and by bringing within his reach some

truth which the angel himself contemplates.

St. Thomas Aquinas (c. 1225–1274)
Sicilian-born Dominican theologian

MUCH ON EARTH IS HIDDEN FROM US, BUT TO MAKE UP FOR

THAT WE HAVE BEEN GIVEN A PRECIOUS MYSTIC SENSE OF OUR LIVING

BOND WITH THE . . . HIGHER HEAVENLY WORLD.

Fyodor Dostoyevsky (1821–1881)
Russian writer

◆

The more materialistic science becomes, the more angels shall I paint:

their wings are my protest in favor of the immortality of the soul.

EDWARD COLEV BURNE-JONES (1833–1889)
ENGLISH ARTIST AND DESIGNER

THE LAST THING I SHOULD EXPECT TO MEET IN HEAVEN

WOULD BE A DEAD LEVEL OF INTELLECT AND TASTE.

I ADMIRE THE NOTION OF SOME OF THE THEOLOGIANS THAT

EACH INDIVIDUAL ANGEL IS A DISTINCT SPECIES IN HIMSELF.

Joseph Farrell (b. 1938)
American academic and writer

Outside the doors of study

 . . . an angel waits.

Hannah Green (b. 1932)
American writer

EVEN THE DARKEST SOUL PASSES,

AT LEAST ONCE IN LIFE, A RAY OF AWARENESS OF THE SUPERNATURAL,

SOMETIMES AT THE BIRTH OF A CHILD OR THE DEATH OF A SOUL.

DAGOBERT D. RUNES (1902–1982)

AMERICAN WRITER

♦

O, BEAUTIFUL RAINBOW, ALL WOVEN OF LIGHT!

HEAVEN SURELY IS OPEN WHEN THOU DOST APPEAR

AND BENDING ABOVE THEE THE ANGELS DRAW NEAR,

AND SING "THE RAINBOW—THE RAINBOW;

THE SMILE OF GOD IS HERE!"

Sarah J. Hale (1790–1879)
American writer and editor

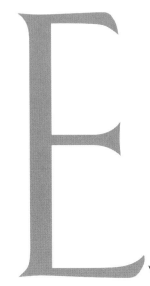

EVERY BREATH OF AIR AND RAY OF LIGHT AND HEAT, EVERY

BEAUTIFUL PROSPECT, IS, AS IT WERE, THE SKIRTS OF THEIR GARMENTS,

THE WAVING OF THE ROBES OF THOSE WHOSE FACES SEE GOD.

John Henry Newman (1801–1890)
English prelate and theologian

DIVINE THINGS

MUST BE LOVED

TO BE KNOWN.

Blaise Pascal (1623–1662)
French scientist and philosopher

◆

ANGELS

LIST OF ILLUSTRATIONS AND PHOTOGRAPHY CREDITS

COVER ART AND P. 44: *Angel* (1889), by Abbott Handerson Thayer (1849–1921). National Museum of American Art, Washington, D.C./Art Resource, New York.

GUARDIANS

P. 8: *Vision of St. Peter Nolasco,* by Francisco de Zurbaran (1598–1664). Museo del Prado, Madrid; Scala/Art Resource, New York.

P. 10: *Madonna and Child with Angels,* by Andrea della Robbia (1435–1525). Duomo, Pistoia, Italy; Scala/Art Resource, New York.

P. 13: *Sacrifice Scene,* by Francesco Fontebasso (1709–1769). Parrochiale, Povo, Italy; Scala/Art Resource, New York.

P. 14: *Adoration of the Shepherds,* by Anton Raphael Mengs (1728–1779). Museo del Prado, Madrid; Scala/Art Resource, New York.

P. 17: *Christ in the Sepulchre, Guarded by Angels,* by William Blake (1757– 1827). Victoria and Albert Museum, London/Bridgeman Art Library, London.

P. 19: *Swing Low Sweet Chariot* (c. 1939), by William H. Johnson (1901– 1970). National Museum of American Art, Washington, D.C./Art Resource, New York.

P. 20: *Tobias and the Angel,* by Jean-Charles Cazin (1841–1901). Musee des Beaux-Arts, Lille, France; Giraudon/Art Resource, New York.

P. 23: Four Angels, detail from *The Madonna of the Magnificat,* by Sandro Botticelli (1445–1510). Uffizi, Florence; Erich Lessing/ Art Resource, New York.

P. 24: *Jacob's Dream (Elie touche par l'ange),* by Marc Chagall (1887–1985); © ARS, New York. Jewish Museum, New York/Art Resource, New York.

P. 27: Detail from *Trinity with St. Ursula and St. Margaret,* by Antonio Maria Viani (c. 1555–1629). Bridgeman Art Library, London.

P. 28: *The Apotheosis of Penelope Boothby,* by Henry Fuseli (1741–1825). Wolverhampton Art Gallery, Staffordshire, Great Britain; Bridgeman Art Library, London.

P. 31: *Angel over Le Besset,* by Michael Chase, 20th-century artist. Private collection/Bridgeman Art Library, London.

ANGELS OF LOVE

P. 32: *The Triumph of Galatea,* by Raphael Sanzio (1483–1520). Palazzo della Farnesina, Rome; Scala/Art Resource, New York.

P. 34: *Three Praying Angels,* by Ridolfo del Ghirlandaio (1483–1561). Accademia, Florence; Scala/Art Resource, New York.

P. 37: *Cupidon* (1891), by William-Adolphe Bouguereau (1825–1905). Roy Miles Gallery, London/Bridgeman Art Library, London.

P. 38: *The Marriage of Cupid (Amore) and Psyche,* by François Boucher (1703–1770). ET Archive, London/Louvre, Paris.

P. 41: *The Fiery Angel* (1927), by Leon Underwood (1890–1975). Phillips, The International Fine Art Auctioneers/Bridgeman Art Library, London.

P. 42: *Angels Rolling Away the Stone from the Sepulchre,* by William Blake (1757–1827). Victoria and Albert Museum, London/Art Resource, New York.

P. 47: *Birth of Venus,* by Alexandre Cabanel (1823–1889). Musee d'Orsay, Paris; Giraudon/Art Resource, New York.

P. 49: *The Poet's Dream,* by Paul Cezanne (1839–1906). Musee d'Orsay, Paris; Giraudon/Art Resource, New York.

P. 50: *The Virgin in Paradise,* by Antoine Auguste Ernest Hébert (1817–1908). Musee Hébert, Paris; Giraudon/Art Resource, New York.

EARTHLY ANGELS

P. 52: *Swarm of Cherubs, a Group of Children in the Sky (L'Essaim d'Amours),* by Jean-Honore Fragonard (1732–1806). Louvre, Paris; Giraudon/Bridgeman Art Library, London.

P. 55: *Head of an Angel,* by Vincent van Gogh (1853–1890). Private collection/Bridgeman Art Library, London.

P. 56: *Madonna of the Village* (1938–1942), by Marc Chagall (1887–1985); © ARS, New York. Thyssen-Bornemisza Museum, Madrid; Scala/Art Resource, New York.

P. 59: *Our Lady of Good Children* (1847–1861), by Ford Madox Brown (1821–1893). Tate Gallery, London/Art Resource, New York.

P. 60: *The Vision* (1924–1925, and c. 1937), by Marc Chagall (1887–1985); © ARS, New York. Tate Gallery, London/Art Resource, New York.

P. 63: Camera degli Sposi, detail from the ceiling of the Palazzo Ducale, by Andrea Mantegna (c. 1431–1506). ET Archive, London/Palazzo Ducale, Mantua, Italy.

P. 65: *Jacob's Ladder* (1973), by Marc Chagall (1887–1985); © ARS, New York. St. Paul de Vence, France; Scala/Art Resource, New York.

P. 66: *The Annunciation,* by Sandro Botticelli (1444–1510). Uffizi, Florence; Scala/Art Resource, New York.

P. 69: Saint Joachim or Joseph, Gothic Hungarian painting (1450), artist unknown. ET Archive, London/National Gallery of Hungarian Art, Budapest.

MUSICAL MESSENGERS

P. 70: *Sacred Music,* by Luigi Mussini (1813–1888). Galleria d'Arte Moderna, Florence; Scala/Art Resource, New York.

P. 73: *Musical Angel,* by Guido Reni (1575–1642). Gabinetto dei Disegni e delle Stampe, Florence; Scala/Art Resource, New York.

P. 74: *Music-making Angel,* by Rosso Fiorentino (1494–1540). Uffizi, Florence; Scala/Art Resource, New York.

P. 76: *Angel,* by Sir Edward Burne-Jones (1833–1898). Private collection/ Bridgeman Art Library, London.

P. 79: Choir of Angels, detail from the *Journey of the Magi* cycle in the chapel of the Palazzo Medici-Riccardi (c. 1460), by Benozzo di Lese Gozzoli di Sandro (1420–1497). Palazzo Medici-Riccardi, Florence/ Bridgeman Art Library, London.

P. 81: *Angel Playing the Violin,* by Melozzo da Forli (1438–1494). Pinacoteca, Vatican Museums, The Vatican; Scala/Art Resource, New York.

P. 82: Angel with Trombone, detail from *The Last Judgement* (c. 1058–1075), artist unknown. St. Angelo in Formis, Capua, Italy; Scala/Art Resource, New York.

P. 85: *Benedicite No. 3 'O Ye Mountains and Hills'* (1899), by Edward A. Fellowes Prynne (1854–1921). Russell-Cotes Art Gallery and Museum, Bournemouth/Bridgeman Art Library, London.

HEAVENLY BEINGS

P. 86: Angel, detail from *The Annunciation,* by Martin Schongauer (c. 1430–1491). ET Archive, London/Unterlinden Museum, Colmar, Germany.

P. 88: *The Glory of Saint Marziale,* by Sebastiano Ricci (1659–1734). St. Marziale, Venice; Cameraphoto/Art Resource, New York .

P. 91: *Two Putti with Scroll,* by Andrea del Sarto (c. 1487–1530). Uffizi, Florence; Scala/Art Resource, New York.

P. 92: *An Angel,* by Valerie Thornton (1931–1991). Private collection/ Bridgeman Art Library, London.

P. 95: *Christmas 77,* by Gillian Lawson, 20th-century artist. Private collection/Bridgeman Art Library, London.

P. 96: *Angels Appearing Before the Shepherds* (c. 1910), by Henry Ossawa Tanner (1859–1937). National Museum of American Art, Washington, D.C./Art Resource, New York.

P. 99: *"How Galahad Sought the Sang Real and Found it because his Heart was Simple so He Followed it to Sarras the City of the Spirit,"* by Sir Edward Burne-Jones (1833–1898). Executed in stained glass by William Morris (1880). Victoria and Albert Museum, London/Art Resource, New York.

P. 100: *Fight between Amors and Bacchic Putti,* by Guido Reni (1575–1642). Galleria Sabauda, Turin, Italy; Scala/Art Resource, New York.

P. 103: *Wounded Angel* (1903), by Hugo Simberg (1873–1917). Konstmuseet i Ateneum, Helsinki/ Bridgeman Art Library, London.

P. 105: *The Cloister or the World* (1896), by Arthur Hacker (1858–1919). Bradford Art Galleries and Museums/Bridgeman Art Library, London.

P. 106: *Putto with a Red Flower,* by Paolo Veronese (c. 1528–1588). The Trustees of the Weston Park Foundation/Bridgeman Art Library, London.

P. 108: *Angel Traveller,* by Gustave Moreau (1826–98). Musee Gustave Moreau, Paris/Bridgeman Art Library, London.

P. 111: *Angels Playing Music,* by Stefano da Verona (1357–1451). ET Archive, London/Correr Museum, Venice.

CELESTIAL MYSTERIES

P. 112: *Madonna of the Adoring Angels,* by Daisy Borne (b. 1906). The collection of Peyton Skipwith; The Fine Art Society, London/Bridgeman Art Library, London.

P. 114: *Angel over Lucca,* by Michael Chase, 20th-century artist. Private collection/Bridgeman Art Library, London.

P. 116: The Two Angels, detail from *The Sistine Madonna,* by Raphael Sanzio (1483–1520). Gemaeldegalerie, Staatliche Kunstsammlungen, Dresden; Erich Lessing/Art Resource, New York.

P. 119: Angels, detail from *The Madonna della Melagrana,* by Sandro Botticelli (1444–1510). Galleria degli Uffizi, Florence/Bridgeman Art Library, London.

P. 120: Detail from the altar of the Lombard King Rachis (c. 700), artist unknown. ET Archive, London/Museo de Duomo, Friuli, Italy.

P. 122: *The Light Shineth in Darkness and the Darkness Comprehendeth It Not,* by Evelyn de Morgan (1850–1919). The De Morgan Foundation, London/ Bridgeman Art Library, London.

P. 125: *The Immaculate Conception,* by Francisco de Zurbaran (1598–1664). ET Archive, London/ Siguenza Guadalajara Dicesan Museum, Siguenza, Spain.

P. 126: *Two Angels,* by Charles Francois Sellier (1830–1882). Private collection; Bridgeman, London/Art Resource, New York.